YOUR RETREATING SHADOW

Roberts

ISBN: 978-1-915079-18-3

Cover designed by Aaron Kent

Edited and typeset by Aaron Kent

Broken Sleep Books Ltd
Rhydwen,
Talgarreg,
SA44 4HB
Wales

Contents

Your Retreating Shadow

Rochelle Roberts

Afterwards

A girl held unstable by a tree, keening
for a stranger who jumped into the ocean,
flesh pooled like a ghost.
A body is a kind of darkness, the smell
of wasted thoughts pumping through water
like a disease.

A girl watching for the haunted body
that drags down the coastline,
a bleak wound beneath the waves.

In the days after she sees, she is hungerless
at a kitchen table. Her eyes sagging-wide,
 an empty structure balancing.

At night the waterlogged body hangs
from her ceiling.
She opens the window but
it cannot fit through.

In the downpour of your absence

we collect our grief in the pockets
of our eyelids as if it might
let us see you again — if only once —
before the inevitable erosion
of memory; the precise vibrations
your voice made through air
or the particular distorted shape
of your body shadow-cast
on the pavement, tiny cracks
in the architecture of you
we have constructed, cracks
that widen and snap so that we
press our fingers to our eyes,
try to keep you intact
but we cannot stop the dissolving.
Fragments slip down our faces,
clutch at our quivering chins
before slipping silently away.

Cyclical

i bite my tongue to wake up
the violence of it
makes me itch
her body cavernous
on the bed
ink-blue and velvety
my grandmother
like a phantom limb
strange wounds grow
in my dreams
drenched streetlamps
my sleep-swollen cheeks
i could disintegrate into
soft bruised skin
between two fingers
like a fish
my body pressed
into
a dream in which i enter

Midsummer

your body opened up

encouraging a
           danger

the forest with small hands

           and dirty teeth

friends who ignored the signs

           who ate the warnings with

           quick fingers

their faces cut-out masks

           sleep-deprived

           skulls

           like stamped on seeds

           insides pulp-soft

she watched

           your bear-furred skin
           burn

her eyes wild triumphant

Margot

She smoked cigarette after
cigarette behind the bike shed
until she disappeared completely
always in white, white dress,
white socks, white shoes, black
cigarettes to match her skin,
small burns on her fingers hidden
by silver rings, white nail-varnish.

I watched her thinking, always her
small face held in a hateful glow.
I hate the feeling but cannot stop.

One night I see her floating above me
in bed, unsmiling. Mr Smith had said
she was hit by a car, that morning
in assembly. I touch her black hair,
her dark mouth, her breast.
At school she had looked at me
with a knowing. I touch her now.
My insides protest.

DWF

On the day you die
you do not get in the car.
You do not sit
in the driver's seat
with heavy-lidded eyes,
the dark streets blurring.
On the motorway
trees slip by like paint-splattering.
You do not close your eyes
to them. The trees wave
goodbye but your car moves
away from the lorry,
your body strapped tight
in the seat, not emerging from
the windscreen
like a puppet, tiny cuts
in the fabric of your skin.
Your face appears
in our family photos,
not scraped along
the cold asphalt.

Night Terror

Your body is not your own
when you bite down on
your tongue, stop the hurt
slipping out,
screams
that fill the womb of my ear
as I press my fingers
to your lips.

There are secrets
hidden in the hallways
of your veins,
dreams that speak
in acid colours.
I watch you dig the skin
of your face,
trying to bury the things
you saw when you were
a child
but they converge in sleep.

I think of what it would be
to feel the weight of you
lying foetal in my skin
or to absorb you
into my marrow.
I hope that it would
give you something to
breathe with, to escape
the imprint of your history
sewn into the whites
of your eyes.

Family History

They found my body swollen between the arms
of a chair, my acid-burned fingers clutching at the hem of my dress.

My sister embedded in the walls, her hair hanging
from her skull in webs, chest open and heartless.

My brother a wound beneath the bathroom sink,
his blood-shot skin coating silver pipes.

They saw my mother as a sorcerer, the ritual
of muttered hexes, her dowsing crystal still in hand.

On the news they showed our faces, headlines bore
no meaning to who we thought we were, ghosts without voices.

We haunt the hallways, haunt the walls
and the garden as our shadows eclipse the moon.

Our faces rubbed purple with grief, the traces
of us no longer in the architecture of our home.

Passive

a   head   hit   repeatedly
   against   a   hard   surface
teeth   like   cracked bones
       the   warm pool   that   collects   in
                              cheeks
         severed   tongue
              lips   soft   and   pulpy
   brimming   with words   that
cannot   find   an   escape
    a   blossom of   violets
                        bluebell
the   string   of   weeds
        that   grows   in   the   pit   of   eyelids

   a   head   on   the   dark   pavement
long   red ribbon   unspooling
        and   behind   the   drawn   curtains
   of   an   overlooking   window
      the   wide   silent   eyes

17

White Boredom

You, with teeth and boredom
arched on my sheets, fingers
stuffed inside as though you think
I might enjoy it.

I pretend to be a hollowed-out
tree, wire mesh around the wound.
Your profile reminds me
of old grievances dropping
from my mouth like loose teeth,
down my spine, between
my legs.

After you fill me up
with your whiteness you
place your fingers on mine
to see how it looks.

This time when you leave quietly
I ignore your retreating shadow.

The Guest Room

thoughts hang
multi-layered
above your bed
creep
from behind
the door in
outlines
of your
childhood self
eyes covered
as though
blinded
by feathered
heat that
rises
from your
mattress
hot little hands
between your
legs
a bruising shame
the smell large
and oaty
pasted on your
skin
bedsheets
sticky soft

Pink Visions

I spy you through a celestial mirror,
your hands flat against the arms
of the metal chair, head on backwards.

The blue curtain swallows you,
the thin fabric of your dress.

I take a pink pill from the jar,
dissolve it between my teeth.
I like the salty taste.

You look beautiful with your face
of hair, silk-shine, copper in sunlight.

I stare until my eyes water, the burn
fills my chest like a monstrous sea.

Your head rotates slowly,
owl-like, milk-blind

the skin on your cheeks red
and feathered as though
I have
hacked them
with
my teeth
but

I am losing
the taste of
blood
rapidly,
translucent
flakes

falling
into my

lap,

the pink
pill the

same
colour

as
the inside
of
your

eyelid.

Stain

there   is   something   that   bleeds
      on   the   mind   in the   dark,
an ink-blue   stain,   spotted   residue
on   the   inside   of   eyelids.
         I   watch   myself   comatose
    on   the   bed,   mouth large   as
         the   insides   of dreams,   eyes
leaking   imagined   horrors,
        all   of   the   words   eating me up

    what if I never wake up
    what if the floor falls open
    what if I was never really here

seeping into   the   crevices of   my brain
      feeding obsession,

           brain
           dead

Lost

You lie with eyes closed, spine
curved, knees tucked up
like a snail's shell or
the shape in which your mother's
finger moves across your palm
tracing a ring of roses.

You fidget in the wake of
exhaustion, dirt-dark beneath
your body, dead leaves pressed
to the exposed strip of skin
between your corduroys and
jumper.

You do not know how long you
have been in this accidental bed.
You feel as though you have lived
an age in black, insects crawling
into the pockets of your trainers,
the scratch of damp in the pit of
your lap.

Beneath the layers of soil,
you do not hear the footsteps
or the crack of her voice left
in the air in front of her.
You do not feel the thick
touch of her gloved hands
as she presses her fingers
into the trunks of trees.

Many times you chose not to
hunt the ghosts on your own.
You were home for dinner,
asleep in your own bed.
She knows that about you.
She knows so much and yet
she cannot feel you beneath
her feet, does not know
you are slipping away.

The Garden

It is daylight when you wake to find you are in the kitchen. Flowers have grown between the floorboards, yellow daisies with fat heads arched towards the window, lavender and honeysuckle casting delicate shadows. Soil covers your bare legs, arm-deep, black behind fingernails, soft with moisture. What a strange dream. A violence. Cigarette smoke through lips, the deep vibrations of a man laughing against the darkness. You thought you felt the warmth of blood on your hands but there is only the earthy smell of plants, roots gripped in your fingers, bruises on your wrists and shoulders, and the recollection of the dream in which you see a face moon-huge in the dark, his small eyes closed. You take a moment to breathe in the chlorophyll, ignore his image, but when you look down to see those blood-soaked fingernails sticking through the soil like stems, it takes you an instant to realise that what is gripped in your hand is not the roots but the handle of a knife.

Grief

The forest, large-eyed and rot-ridden. Leaves open up like lungs as I walk from the path into the dark teeth of trees. The taste of burning rises in the shape of ghosts, my shadow like grit between branches. I touch tree trunks. They leave a violent stain.

I want to escape these thoughts polluted with dead language. Syllables that fall into empty space. The trees are haunted by the mistakes of generations, a grief that cannot be articulated into meaning. I let it fall from beneath my tongue. I want to burn with the forest, to feel some part of it. I want to bury my grief in the acidic soil, water it until something clean grows.

Summer

In the kitchen screams come from the cracks between the tiles,
the sound pouring onto the white floor as though they have
peeled open their insides. In the dim, they are ghosts. Their

incantations balloon me,
cracks look like tiny people,
the white tiled walls. I hate to
the screaming burning my
eyelashes. I beat my fists
cracks shatter and the faces
nothing but my fists and the red

bleeding from my ears. The
the image of my face against
look but they are everywhere,
mouth, my face wet with
against the tiles until the
fall away, until there is
sliding down the walls.

Accidental Sleep

deep-rooted,
the feeling of
             slipping
body heavy, throbbing
behind eyes
             insignificant pains
             manifesting as disaster
exhaustion pulling me
into the disappearance of sleep
a fear
   of not waking up
   confusion of shifting states
                  tight chest
my body melting
into an unnoticed darkness
slowed breathing
             and then

                  the brightness of sunrise
                  the forgetting of fears

Hôtel du Pavot

After Room 202, Hôtel du Pavot by Dorothea Tanning

I stand   keening   outside
                room 202 as if
        to cast spells, reverse the outcome,
        walls   dark with   patterns
                from   monstrous   trees
        bending   spines
                        through the   open   window.

                The door stands ajar
        framing   the room   with
        the   light   from a   naked bulb,
antique wallpaper
        clutching   at the   rotting   walls.

                The   room   sweats   bodies
                that   sag
        as   though   birthed   from   wounds,
        bodies   climbing out
                        of   the   fireplace,
                from   between   the limbs   of chairs,
        their   outlines   with   arms
                and   legs   that   twist   away,
                                        headless.

        On   the   floor in   the   centre,
        the   stain   of   me,   head   weeping
        into   a   pool,   evidence   of witchery.
I   stand   with   my mouth   black
                                        with tears,
                the   bodies
        that   smother   mine.
                        A painful regret.

Useless Magic

colours that smell
of the deathening point
at which black is
chewed up between
hungry teeth

we did not kill our fathers
but watched them sink
beneath the thumb of land
their orphaned fingers
risen like dead sticks

red mould grew
from the wound
of their graves
blood puckering
between cracks

we say the necessary spells
casting shadows
over our own faces
matchbox fires
burn at our feet
but still the uncontrollable
red polluting the air
like a sickness

leaves grow from the soil
in the outline of bodies
we know to be our fathers'
we do not dare
to cut back the disease
their bodies glossy as honey
drooping in the sun
mouths gaping
as though they can still

feel the hunger of those colours
growing in crescent shapes
around their heads
just before their collapse

we watch the blood
of our fathers boiling
through the earth
the leaves the shape
of their ghosts
the black jewels
that glitter in the heat
of those crescent shaped
colours now burning
above our heads

our small spines bend
with the joints in our legs
we smell the colours
as we press our faces
to the earth
the hunger we try to bury
in acid
the colours that ate our fathers
in one sagging bite
black jewels between
our shrivelled fingers
small and cosmic
like the pupils of eyes
black jewels pressed to
our lips before we know how
to stop ourselves
crunch down
with hungry teeth
knowing that tomorrow
there will be no trance
just the sun
honeyed leaves
and our useless incantations
extinguished

Acknowledgements

To Joe, Toni and Shannon
and to my parents and Tia for all of the love and support.

To Sammy for making me start writing poetry again, and for being the best poet friend. And to Verity, Nic, Sophia, Helena and Katy. I am so grateful for our little poetry family. To Alice and the stanza group for all the help and encouragement, and for being brilliant readers and editors of many of these poems. To Rebecca for the early belief in my work. And to Aaron for publishing me.

To the magazines and presses who published some of these poems: Tentacular, Perverse, Severine and Takeaway Press & 3 of Cups Press.

To the artists whose work inspired some of these poems: Dorothea Tanning, Gregory Crewdson, Anja Niemi.

And to everyone who reads this book. Thank you.

LAY OUT YOUR UNREST

Lightning Source UK Ltd.
Milton Keynes UK
UKHW012302090922
408592UK00001B/35